TIM TEBOW

BY ALEX MONNIG

Published by ABDO Publishing Company, PO Box 398166, Minneapolis, MN 55439.
Copyright © 2013 by Abdo Consulting Group, Inc. International copyrights reserved in all
countries. No part of this book may be reproduced in any form without written permission
from the publisher. SportsZone™ is a trademark and logo of ABDO Publishing Company.

Printed in the United States of America,
North Mankato, Minnesota
052012
092012

 THIS BOOK CONTAINS AT LEAST 10% RECYCLED MATERIALS.

Editor: Chrös McDougall
Series Designer: Craig Hinton

Photo Credits: Paul Spinelli/AP Images, cover, 1; Dave Martin/AP Images, 4; Phelan
M. Ebenhack/AP Images, 7; Eric Gay/AP Images, 8; Tom DiPace/AP Images, 11; Jamie
Schwaberow/NCAA Photos/AP Images, 13; John Raoux/AP Images, 14, 19; Kelly Kline/AP
Images, 16; John Bazemore/AP Images, 21; Eric Bakke/AP Images, 22; Julie Jacobson/AP
Images, 24; Thomas E. Witte/AP Images, 27; David Drapkin/AP Images, 29

Library of Congress Cataloging-in-Publication Data
Monnig, Alex.
  Tim Tebow : quarterback sensation / Alex Monnig.
     p. cm. -- (Playmakers)
  Includes index.
  ISBN 978-1-61783-550-6
  1. Tebow, Tim, 1987- 2. Football players--United States--Biography. 3. Quarterbacks
(Football)--United States--Biography. I. Title.
  GV939.T423M66 2013
  796.332092--dc23
  [B]
                                      2012008242

TABLE OF CONTENTS

Tim Tebow

CHAPTER 1

DETERMINED EFFORT

Tim Tebow was only a college junior in 2008. Yet he was already the quarterback and leader of the Florida Gators football team. The Gators were one of the country's best teams. Tim and his teammates set lofty goals for the season. They wanted to win every game. No Florida team had ever done that. They also wanted to win the national championship.

Tim Tebow never gave up during Florida's 2008 national championship season.

Then, Ole Miss upset Florida 31–30 in the fourth game that season. It looked like the Gators had blown their chance at the national title. Tim was upset. He almost cried at the press conference after the game. But he was not ready to give up. He apologized to the fans. Then he promised to work harder than any other player in college football and lead the team. And that is just what he did.

The Gators did not lose another game that season. They beat Alabama in the conference title game. Then they beat Oklahoma 24–14 in the national championship game. Tim passed for 231 yards and two touchdowns. He also rushed for 109 yards. Tim had kept his promise.

Tim's faith in himself and his teammates came from his family. He was born on August 14, 1987, in Manila, Philippines. His parents had moved to that country from the United States

Tim has two older sisters, Christy and Katie, and two older brothers, Robby and Peter. His parents, Bob and Pam, are also graduates of Florida. They run a ministry called the Bob Tebow Evangelistic Association.

Members of Tim's family look on as Tim addresses the media following the 2010 NFL Draft.

two years earlier. They did missionary work through their church. Tim's parents shared strong Christian beliefs. They passed their religious beliefs on to Tim and his four older siblings.

Tim's family moved back to Jacksonville, Florida, when Tim was three years old. All of the Tebow kids were homeschooled through high school. That meant their parents taught them at home instead of sending them to a school. But Tim still found himself at high school often. That is because he played for his local high school's football team.

CHAPTER 2

LOCAL STAR

Tebow played one season at Trinity Christian Academy. But he was on defense. So in 2003 he began playing as a quarterback at Nease High School in Jacksonville. Some people were surprised. Nease's football team had struggled the year before. That would soon change.

Tebow started at quarterback all three years he was at Nease. During that time, he set several Florida high school records. Among the records were career

Tebow drives into an opposing player during a high school all-star game in January 2006.

passing yards (9,940), total yards (12,960), completed passes (631), and total touchdowns (159).

Tebow shined as a dual-threat quarterback. That meant he was great at passing and rushing the football. He rushed for 3,169 yards and 63 touchdowns during his time there. As a senior in 2005, he helped lead Nease to its first state title.

Tebow was a high school star. Many colleges wanted him to come play football for their teams. Tebow narrowed his choices to two schools: Florida and Alabama. Both schools have powerhouse football teams. But in the end, Tebow decided to stay closer to home. He enrolled at Florida in January 2006.

The Gators were traditionally one of the best football teams in the country. As such, they brought in a lot of top-rated players. Tebow was a local legend at Nease. But at Florida, he had to earn a starting role just like everybody else.

Tebow earned a lot of awards in high school. He was first-team All-State in 2004 and 2005. He was also named a Parade All-American for the 2005 season. That is one of the highest honors a high school football player can receive.

THE SWAMP
ONLY GATORS GET OUT ALIVE

Tebow decided to stay closer to home after high school and play college football for the Florida Gators.

Senior Chris Leak was Florida's quarterback in 2006. He had been the starter since his freshman year. So Leak remained Florida's main quarterback during Tebow's freshman year. Tebow still got on the field, though.

Tebow's size and running ability made him hard to defend. So Florida coach Urban Meyer regularly brought him in to keep defenses on their toes. Tebow had some success passing the ball. He completed 22 of his 33 passes that year. Among those were five touchdowns and only one interception. But it was as a runner that Tebow really helped the Gators. He ran 89 times for 469 yards and eight touchdowns. He had the second most rushing yards on the team.

The Gators lost just once all season. That earned them a berth into the national championship game. There they met the Ohio State Buckeyes. The Buckeyes scored on the opening kickoff to take an early 7–0 lead. But they would only score once more after that. Florida walked away with a 41–14 victory and the national championship.

Tebow only threw one pass in the national championship game. But it was an important one. The freshman came on with 23 seconds left in the third quarter. The Gators were on the Ohio State 1-yard line with a 27–14 lead. The Buckeyes' defenders did not know whether Tebow would run or pass the ball.

As a freshman, Tebow scored a touchdown in seven of Florida's 14 games. But one game stood out from the rest. Tebow threw for 200 yards and two touchdowns against Western Carolina. He also ran for 47 yards and another two touchdowns. Florida easily won the game 62–0.

Tebow prepares to throw a touchdown pass during the national championship game after the 2006 season.

Indeed, Tebow threw it. His one-yard touchdown pass to junior wide receiver Andre Caldwell put away the game.

The Gators found themselves back on the 1-yard line with 10:20 remaining in the fourth quarter. Once again, Meyer went to Tebow. And once again, the Gators came away with a touchdown. This time Tebow ran the ball in for the score.

Tebow was not Florida's starting quarterback. But he had played a major role in the team's success as a freshman. Fans were excited for the next season. With Leak gone, Tebow would take over as the Gators' starting quarterback.

Tim Tebow

CHAPTER 3

TEBOW TAKES OVER

The Gators fell short of a second national championship in 2007. Yet Tebow still led the team to a solid 9–4 record in his first year as starting quarterback.

Florida's offense was the driving force behind many of those wins. And Tebow was the driving force behind the offense. The sophomore threw for 3,286 yards and 32 touchdowns. He also ran for 895 yards and 23 touchdowns. College football is divided

With Chris Leak gone, Tebow became Florida's starting quarterback for the 2007 season.

Tim Tebow

among several divisions. Tebow became the first player in the top division to throw for 20 touchdowns and rush for 20 touchdowns in the same season. His 23 rushing touchdowns were also a Southeastern Conference (SEC) record.

Each year, the Heisman Trophy is awarded to the best player in college football. The winner had always been a junior or a senior. But Tebow changed that. He became the first sophomore Heisman Trophy winner.

Tebow was already well known for his football skills. He was also becoming well known off the field. Like his parents, Tebow was passionate about charity work. While at Florida, he often donated his time to speak at schools. He even visited a prison once to share what he had learned from his family.

Tebow had high expectations for his junior season. After the loss to Ole Miss and Tebow's post-game speech, the Gators lived up to them. They won their second national championship in three years.

In 2007, Tebow became the first sophomore to win the Heisman Trophy.

In just three seasons, Tebow had rushed for 43 touchdowns. No player in Florida history had that many in his career. Some Florida fans worried Tebow would never add to that record. That is because players can enter the National Football League (NFL) Draft three years after graduating from high school. But Tebow decided to stay at Florida for his senior year. He wanted to win another national championship.

The Gators were one of the favorites to win a national title going into the 2009 season. They started the year 12–0. That helped them earn a spot in the SEC championship game against the Alabama Crimson Tide.

Florida came into the game ranked number one. But Alabama was also undefeated and ranked number two. That meant the winner of the game would get a chance to play for the national championship.

While at Florida, Tebow and several other students started a foundation called First and 15. It helped students and other Florida supporters organize time and money for various charities.

Tebow finds a hole to run through during a 2009 game against Florida International.

It turned out to be Alabama's year. The Crimson Tide beat the Gators 32–13. Tebow's dream of a third national title was over. But Florida regrouped to crush Cincinnati 51–24 in the Sugar Bowl. Tebow played very well in his final college game. He threw for 482 yards and three touchdowns. He also rushed for 51 yards and one touchdown.

Many great football players have worn the Florida Gators' colors throughout the years. Tebow left the school as perhaps its best player ever. He had become the first sophomore to win the Heisman Trophy. And he was a finalist for the award as a junior and senior. Tebow also left Florida with dozens of records. He had five national records, 14 SEC records, and 28 Florida records.

Perhaps what Florida fans will remember the most about Tebow, though, was the Gators' success during his four years there. Tebow helped the team win two national championships. The Gators had only won one prior to his arrival.

College success does not always carry over to the NFL, though. Tebow thrived as a dual-threat quarterback in Florida's wide-open offense. But it is much harder for a quarterback to

Tebow left Florida with several SEC career records. Among them were pass completion percentage (66.4) and rushing touchdowns (57). He tied with Chris Leak for career touchdown passes (88).

Tebow passes over the Alabama defensive line during the 2009 SEC Championship Game.

run the football in the NFL. Some wondered if Tebow's passing abilities were good enough for the NFL. All Tebow wanted was an opportunity to prove those people wrong.

Tim Tebow

CHAPTER 4

DENVER DAYS

Tebow was one of the biggest college football stars ever. Many fans were interested to see where he would end up in the NFL Draft. Some thought he would go in the first round. Others doubted Tebow. They thought he would fall much lower. The Denver Broncos did not doubt him.

The Broncos traded their second, third, and fourth-round picks to obtain the twenty-fifth selection in the draft. Then they chose Tebow with that pick.

The Denver Broncos traded up to select Tebow with the twenty-fifth pick in the 2010 NFL Draft.

Tebow greets a young fan prior to a 2011 game against the Chicago Bears.

Tebow had indeed gone in the first round. Denver already had quarterbacks Kyle Orton and Brady Quinn. But the team believed in Tebow.

Like at Florida, Tebow did not walk into a starting role. He played in nine games during his rookie year. However, he did not see much playing time until the end of the year. The Broncos started the season 2–2. Then they lost eight of their next nine games. With nothing to lose, the team let Tebow start the final three games.

The Broncos beat the Houston Texans 24–23 in Tebow's second game as a starter. Tebow threw for one touchdown. He also ran for one touchdown in the fourth quarter. The Broncos earned a comeback victory. It would not be his last.

Tebow was hardly an NFL star from his play on the field. Yet he was already one of the most popular players in the league. Many people had loved watching Tebow while he was at Florida. Also, many people liked that Tebow was so open about his Christian beliefs. They appreciated that he was true to himself.

Despite his popularity, Tebow was again a backup to start the next season. But the Broncos continued to struggle. With Orton starting, Denver got off to a 1–3 start. The team

Denver wide receiver Eddie Royal went down with an injury during the Broncos' second game of the 2011 season. Tebow was called in to be the team's emergency third wide receiver.

appeared on its way to another loss the next week. The Broncos trailed the San Diego Chargers 23–10 at halftime. So the coaches decided to start Tebow in the second half.

Tebow led the Broncos to two touchdowns in the fourth quarter. The Chargers still won, 29–24. But Tebow had shown a lot of leadership in his play. So the Broncos decided to start him for their next game.

Tebow got off to a bad start on the road against the Miami Dolphins. The Broncos found themselves down 15–0 with 5:23 left in the fourth quarter. But Tebow did not give up. He then completed 9 of 13 passes for 121 yards and two touchdowns. His second touchdown pass sent the game into overtime. The Broncos were able to kick a field goal in overtime to win.

The Detroit Lions destroyed the Broncos 45–10 the next week. But then something began to change. The Broncos

With Tebow's success in 2011, he also became more popular. His jersey was the twenty-fourth most purchased among fans in September. By the end of November, it had moved to number two. Only Green Bay Packers quarterback Aaron Rodgers was higher.

Tebow takes a snap during a 2011 game against the San Diego Chargers.

began winning. Soon they had won six straight games. And the more the Broncos won, the more people began paying attention to Tebow.

Fans and media members tried to pinpoint the reason behind Tebow's success. In several of those wins, Tebow and the Broncos began very slowly. Then, as time was running out, something would click. Tebow became a fourth-quarter star. The Broncos came from behind in six of Tebow's seven wins.

Tebow helped write a biography called *Through My Eyes*. It was released on May 31, 2011. The book is about the ups and downs of his time playing at Florida. It debuted at number six on the *New York Times* hardcover nonfiction bestseller list.

Denver lost its final three games of the season. But at 8–8, the team still qualified for the playoffs. Fans in Denver were excited. The Broncos had not hosted a playoff game since 2005.

Still, many wrote off Tebow and the Broncos after their late-season skid. Plus, the Broncos had to host the Pittsburgh Steelers in the playoffs. Pittsburgh had been in the Super Bowl the year before. But Tebow had shown that he should never be written off—especially late in games. As it turned out, the game went into overtime. And Tebow hit wide receiver Demaryius Thomas for an 80-yard touchdown on the first play. Once again, Tebow led the team to a late victory.

Tebow was again the sensation of the NFL. But the exciting season ended the next week. The Broncos were crushed 45–10 on the road against the powerful New England Patriots.

Changes were in store for Tebow. After the season, the Broncos signed legendary quarterback Peyton Manning and

After Tebow's breakout 2011 season, the Jets hoped he could continue his winning ways in New York.

traded Tebow to the New York Jets. The move created quite a stir. Tebow was already one of the NFL's most popular players. Now he was playing in the country's biggest city. Tebow would also have to work with the Jets' other young quarterback, Mark Sanchez. But the Jets believed in Tebow. As Tebow had shown throughout his career, with him on the field, his team would always have a chance to win.

FUN FACTS AND QUOTES

- Tim Tebow showed his fighting spirit before he was even born. His mother had to take some medication before she knew she was pregnant with Tim. Doctors said that the medication had affected the baby, and that it might not even survive birth. But Tim and his mother both came through healthy.

- Tebow's toughness was also on display during his sophomore year at Nease High School. He hurt his leg early in a game that season, but he played on. He even tied the game with a 29-yard touchdown run in the fourth quarter. An X-ray after the game showed that his leg was broken.

- *"To the fans and everybody in Gator Nation, I'm sorry. . . . I promise you one thing, a lot of good will come out of this. You will never see any player in the entire country play as hard as I will play the rest of the season. You will never see someone push the rest of the team as hard as I will push everybody the rest of the season. You will never see a team play harder than we will the rest of the season. God bless."* —Tebow after Florida's 2008 loss to Ole Miss

- Tebow's last game with Florida was on January 1, 2010. But his influential words live on there. A plaque at the entrance of the Florida Field football facility shares his speech after the 2008 loss to Ole Miss.

WEB LINKS

To learn more about Tim Tebow, visit ABDO Publishing Company online at **www.abdopublishing.com**. Web sites about Tebow are featured on our Book Links page. These links are routinely monitored and updated to provide the most current information available.

GLOSSARY

charity

Money given or work done to help people in need.

conference

In sports, a group of teams that plays each other each season.

draft

A system used by professional sports leagues to select new players in order to spread incoming talent among all teams. The NFL Draft is held each spring.

drive

When a team on offense moves down the field.

dual-threat

When a quarterback is good at both running and passing the ball.

interception

A pass thrown by a quarterback that is caught by a member of the opposing defense.

ministry

A religious group that serves others.

missionary

A person who does volunteer work on behalf of a religion.

overtime

An extra session of football played when a game is tied after four regulation periods.

rookie

A first-year player in the NFL.

upset

A result where the supposedly worse team defeats the supposedly better team.

INDEX

FURTHER RESOURCES

Dooley, Pat. *Florida Gators Football: Yesterday & Today*. Lincolnwood, IL: West Side, 2009.

Gitlin, Marty. *Florida Gators*. Minneapolis, MN: ABDO Publishing Co., 2013.

Tebow, Tim. *Through My Eyes: A Quarterback's Journey, Young Reader's Edition*. Grand Rapids, MI: Zondervan, 2011.